**This book provided
through funds from the
City of Portland**

1997-1998

from SEA TO SHINING SEA
TENNESSEE

By Dennis Brindell Fradin

CONSULTANTS

James A. Hoobler, Curator of Art & Architecture, Tennessee State Museum;
former Executive Director, Tennessee Historical Society

Robert L. Hillerich, Ph.D., Consultant, Pinellas County Schools, Florida;
Visiting Professor, University of South Florida

CHILDRENS PRESS®
CHICAGO

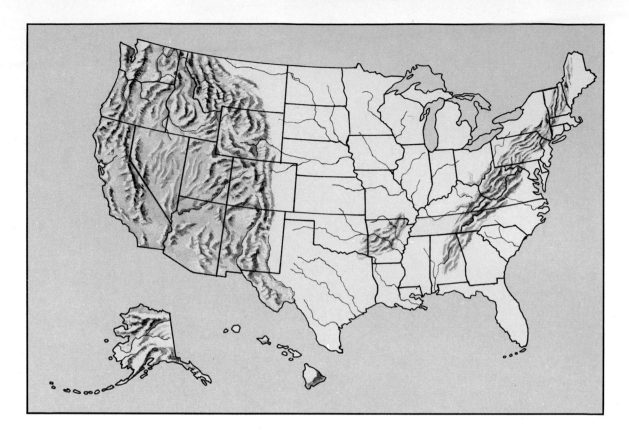

Tennessee is one of the fourteen states in the region called the South. The other southern states are Alabama, Arkansas, Delaware, Florida, Georgia, Kentucky, Louisiana, Maryland, Mississippi, North Carolina, South Carolina, Virginia, and West Virginia.

For Marilyn Choll

For her help, the author thanks Nancy Sevier Madden

Front cover picture, Knoxville; page 1, a herd of horses grazing in Cades Cove, Great Smoky Mountains National Park; back cover, Laurel Falls

Project Editor: Joan Downing

Design Director: Karen Kohn

Typesetting: Graphic Connections, Inc.

Engraving: Liberty Photoengraving

Library of Congress Cataloging-in-Publication Data

Fradin, Dennis B.
  Tennessee / by Dennis Brindell Fradin.
    p.   cm. — (From sea to shining sea)
  Includes index.
  Summary: An overview of the Volunteer State, introducing its history, geography, industries, sites of interest, and famous people.
  ISBN 0-516-03842-7
  1. Tennessee—Juvenile literature. [1. Tennessee.]
I. Title. II. Series: Fradin, Dennis B. From sea to shining sea.
F436.3.F68   1992   92-6385
976.8—dc20   CIP
                                             AC

A Nashville family on a summer weekend

Table of Contents

DUNNINGTON

Introducing the Volunteer State

*T*ennessee is one of the fourteen southern states. It was named for *Tanasie,* a Cherokee Indian village. Creek and Chickasaw Indians also once lived in Tennessee.

Tennesseans helped build the young United States. Frontiersman Davy Crockett was born in Tennessee. Andrew Jackson, James Polk, and Andrew Johnson were Tennessee lawmakers. These three men became presidents of the United States.

Tennesseans have always been quick to serve in wartime. Many volunteered during the War of 1812. That is why Tennessee is called the

A picture map of Tennessee

"Volunteer State." Tennessean Alvin York was a hero in World War I.

Today, Tennessee is a modern state. Scientists in Tennessee helped create the atomic bomb. Chemicals and other goods are made in Tennessee's cities. Tennessee is the birthplace of much modern popular music.

There is much more that is special about the Volunteer State. Where is Graceland, the home of singer Elvis Presley? What state has a big lake that was formed by earthquakes? What state is most famous for country music? Where were Indian leader Sequoya and singer Dolly Parton born? The answer to these questions is: Tennessee!

Overleaf: Bald cypress trees at Reelfoot National Wildlife Refuge

5

A Star for Each Region

A Star for Each Region

T ennessee is shaped like a finger pointing east. The fingertip lies in the Appalachian Mountains. The finger's base touches the Mississippi River.

The Volunteer State is in the region called the South. Eight other states border Tennessee. Kentucky and Virginia are to the north. North Carolina is to the east. Georgia, Alabama, and Mississippi are to the south. Arkansas and Missouri are to the west.

Besides Tennessee, the only state with eight neighbors is Missouri.

Geography

There are three stars on the Tennessee flag. Each star stands for a region of Tennessee. Tennesseans divide their state into three regions. They are East, Middle, and West Tennessee.

East Tennessee is mountainous. The Appalachian Mountains form Tennessee's eastern

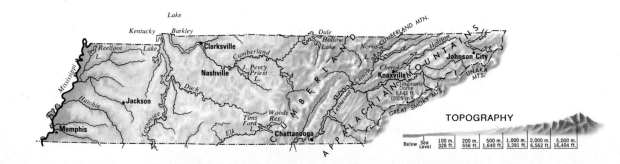

TOPOGRAPHY

| Below Sea Level | 100 m. 328 ft. | 200 m. 656 ft. | 500 m. 1,640 ft. | 1,000 m. 3,281 ft. | 2,000 m. 6,562 ft. | 5,000 m. 16,404 ft. |

border. A famous range in Tennessee's Appalachians is the Great Smoky Mountains. Clingmans Dome is found in those mountains. It is Tennessee's highest peak at 6,643 feet. Chattanooga and Knoxville are East Tennessee's largest cities.

Middle Tennessee is hilly in places. It also has vast stretches of flat land. That land is cut here and there by river valleys. The Central Basin is in the heart of Middle Tennessee. This is a hilly area. It is shaped somewhat like a bowl. Nashville is in the Central Basin. It is Tennessee's capital and second-largest city.

West Tennessee is part of the Gulf Coastal Plain. It is made up mostly of low flatlands. Those flatlands are sometimes broken up by hills and valleys. Far western Tennessee has some of the state's best

Wild blue phlox (right) is one of the many wildflowers that grow in the Great Smoky Mountains (left).

Half of the state of Tennessee is wooded.

soil. It is found along the Mississippi River. Memphis lies on the Mississippi River in Tennessee's far southwestern corner. Memphis is Tennessee's largest city.

RIVERS, LAKES, WOODS, AND WILDLIFE

The Mississippi River is 2,340 miles long. The Tennessee River is 652 miles long. The Cumberland River is 720 miles long.

Tennessee's western border is squiggly. That is because the Mississippi River forms the border. The Mississippi is the United States' longest river. The Cumberland and the Tennessee are the state's two other main rivers. The Cumberland flows across northern Middle Tennessee. Tennessee has been called the "Big Bend State." The Tennessee River bends through it like a *U*.

Many dams have been built on the Tennessee and Cumberland rivers. Those dams have created beautiful lakes. The biggest of those lakes in Tennessee is Kentucky Lake. It is at the western Kentucky-Tennessee border.

Reelfoot Lake is Tennessee's biggest natural lake. Reelfoot is young. In 1811-12, earthquakes rocked northwest Tennessee and nearby areas. The land sank in places due to the quakes. Mississippi River water rushed in at one such place. That's how Reelfoot Lake was formed.

Half of Tennessee is wooded. Hickories, oaks, and pines are important trees in Tennessee. Elms,

The Little Pigeon River (left) flows through Great Smoky Mountains National Park. Trilliums (right) thrive in the state's wooded areas.

*Bald eagles (above left) and raccoons (below) make their home in Tennessee.
Fall colors brighten the landscape (above right).*

maples, and walnuts are common in the state. The tulip poplar is the state tree.

Bears share the Tennessee woodlands with deer, rabbits, raccoons, and foxes. Wild hogs live in the mountains. Many kinds of birds nest in Tennessee. They include mockingbirds (the state bird), cardinals, robins, and eagles.

CLIMATE

Tennessee's climate is warm. Summer temperatures above 80 degrees Fahrenheit are common in

Tennessee. That is warm. But it's not as hot as it often gets in states farther south.

Winter temperatures often approach 50 degrees Fahrenheit. Tennessee's yearly snowfall is low. About 12 inches fall in the East Tennessee mountains. Half that amount falls in West Tennessee.

Tennessee sometimes is hurt by disasters such as floods and tornadoes. The Mississippi River flood of 1937 left thousands of families homeless. Floods occurred again in 1983. Tornadoes sometimes touch down around Memphis. Three people died in a tornado in May 1995.

A winter snowfall coats the banks of the Pigeon River.

From Ancient Times Until Today

From Ancient Times Until Today

Millions of years ago, seas covered Tennessee. Seashells have been found on what is now dry land.

Some animals that no longer exist lived in Tennessee in ancient times. There were mammoths and mastodons. These huge animals were related to present-day elephants. Saber-toothed tigers also roamed through Tennessee.

American Indians

Ancient Indians reached Tennessee about 15,000 years ago. About 1,000 years ago, American Indians began building dirt mounds. Some mounds held the bones of the dead. Others supported temples and homes. One of the Pinson Mounds is seven stories tall. It is in southwest Tennessee.

By the 1500s, three main Indian tribes lived in Tennessee. The Cherokees lived in the East. The Creeks lived in the Southeast. The Chickasaws lived in the West.

The Indians grew corn in fields near their houses. They hunted deer and wild turkeys in the woods.

Opposite: Homestead cabin, Great Smoky Mountains National Park

EUROPEAN EXPLORERS AND TRADERS

Three European countries hoped to rule North America. They were Spain, France, and England. All three sent explorers to Tennessee.

Hernando De Soto of Spain was the first known European in Tennessee. He arrived in 1540. De Soto and his men raided Indian villages in Tennessee. In 1542, De Soto died. The Spaniards then left Tennessee.

In 1673, other Europeans arrived. They were Englishmen James Needham and Gabriel Arthur. Needham and Arthur explored the eastern Tennessee River valley. Also in 1673, two Frenchmen canoed down the Mississippi River. They were Louis Jolliet and Father Jacques Marquette. Their route took them down what is now Tennessee's western border.

In 1682, another French explorer claimed the Mississippi Valley for France. His name was René-Robert Cavelier, Sieur de La Salle. La Salle built a fort that overlooked the Mississippi River. In 1714, Charles Charleville built a fur-trading post. It stood at French Lick. That was near present-day Nashville.

English fur traders also arrived. The French and English traded with the Indians. The Indians

Frenchman Father Jacques Marquette explored the Mississippi River.

16

received guns and pots in return for animal furs. The furs were shipped to Europe. There, they were made into clothing.

ENGLAND CONTROLS TENNESSEE

In 1754, England and France began the French and Indian War. It was for the control of North America. In Tennessee, the Creeks fought for the French. The Cherokees and Chickasaws sided with the English. England won this war in 1763. England gained control of most of the land east of the Mississippi, including Tennessee. The Tennessee region was made part of England's North Carolina colony. By that time, England had thirteen colonies along the Atlantic Ocean.

Tennessee's first known settler was William Bean. Bean was from North Carolina. In 1769, he built a cabin in eastern Tennessee.

By 1770, Tennessee had about 1,000 settlers. All of them lived near the Watauga River. Those settlers formed the Watauga Association in 1772. It was one of colonial America's first examples of self-government.

It was hard for settlers to cross the mountains into Tennessee. North Carolinian Daniel Boone

Daniel Boone (above) blazed the Wilderness Trail through the Cumberland Gap so settlers could cross the mountains into Tennessee.

helped solve this problem. In 1775, Boone blazed the Wilderness Road. It went through the Cumberland Gap. Thousands of pioneers took this road to Tennessee and Kentucky.

BECOMING THE SIXTEENTH STATE

Jonesborough was founded in East Tennessee in 1779. In 1779-80, settlers under James Robertson and John Donelson built Fort Nashborough in Middle Tennessee. It later became Nashville.

Meanwhile, the American colonists were fighting for their independence from England. This was called the Revolutionary War (1775-1783). Tennesseans under John Sevier and Isaac Shelby helped win the Battle of Kings Mountain in South Carolina, on October 7, 1780.

The American victory at Kings Mountain helped America win the war in 1781. The peace treaty was signed in 1783. The thirteen colonies had become the United States of America. But Tennessee was still part of North Carolina.

Many eastern Tennesseans refused to be ruled by lawmakers in faraway North Carolina. In 1784, eastern Tennesseans founded their own state, called Franklin. John Sevier was elected governor.

*Jonesborough (above)
was founded in 1779.*

*The state of Franklin
was named for the
famous Benjamin
Franklin of
Pennsylvania.*

18

Franklin did not last long as a state. In 1788, Franklin again became part of North Carolina. In 1789, North Carolina gave Tennessee to the United States government. Tennessee was then made a United States territory. That was a big step toward statehood.

By 1796, Tennessee had about 80,000 settlers. That was more than enough people for statehood. Congress made Tennessee the sixteenth state on June 1, 1796. Knoxville was the first state capital. John Sevier was elected the state's first governor.

Tennesseans under John Sevier (right) and Isaac Shelby helped win the Battle of Kings Mountain (left).

THE YOUNG STATE

The young state of Tennessee grew quickly. Between 1800 and 1820, Tennessee's population

Andrew Jackson (above) was president from 1829 to 1837.

jumped from 105,602 to 422,828. Settlers came from other states and from Europe.

From 1812 to 1815, America fought the War of 1812 against England. Thousands of Tennesseans volunteered to fight in this war. That was when Tennessee earned its nickname, the "Volunteer State." Tennessee's Andrew Jackson became a hero of this war. With help from many Tennesseans, Jackson won the war's last battle. It was at New Orleans in 1815.

In 1828, Jackson was elected the seventh president of the United States. Jackson was a great president in many ways. He was a friend of farmers and workers. But he was no friend to the Indians. Jackson sided with the white people who wanted to settle on Indian lands.

The Cherokees were sure they wouldn't be forced off their land. They had their own schools. They printed their own books. They used an alphabet devised by their great leader Sequoya. But the Cherokees were pushed to Oklahoma during the 1830s. Many Indians died on the way. That trip became known as the "Trail of Tears."

Another group of Tennesseans was also suffering. Tennessee allowed slavery. Many Middle Tennessee families owned several slaves. They took care of tobacco and other crops. Some rich families in West Tennessee owned huge farms called plantations. Slaves planted and picked cotton crops on the plantations. By 1840, 183,057 of Tennessee's 829,210 people were black slaves.

Slavery had never been widespread in the North. By 1820, it had been ended there. The North wanted the South to end slavery, too. The argument over slavery went on for many years. In the midst of it, James Polk of Tennessee was elected president in 1844. From 1845 to 1849, President Polk improved the country in many ways. During his term, the United States fought the Mexican War. The Volunteer State sent about 30,000 men. They helped win this war. California and other western lands were added to the United States. But the eleventh president did not try to end slavery.

Tennessean James Polk (above) was president from 1845 to 1849.

THE CIVIL WAR

Abraham Lincoln was elected president in 1860. The southern states feared that he would end slavery. One by one, they left the United States. They formed their own country. Its name was the Confederate States of America. It was called the Confederacy for short.

During the Civil War, these black troops fought against the Confederacy at Nashville.

War between the Confederacy (the South) and the Union (the North) began on April 12, 1861. This was the start of the Civil War (1861-1865). Tennessee joined the Confederacy on June 8, 1861.

Many Tennessee families were divided over the war. About 125,000 Tennesseans fought for the Confederacy. Another 70,000 fought for the Union. These Union troops included about 20,000 black Tennesseans. Most of them were escaped slaves.

Hundreds of Civil War battles took place in Tennessee. They included two of the deadliest battles ever fought in America. The Battle of Shiloh was fought on April 6-7, 1862. About 13,000

Only Virginia had more big Civil War battles than Tennessee.

Union and 11,000 Confederate troops were killed or wounded. The Battle of Murfreesboro (or Stones River) began on the last day of 1862. It ended on January 2, 1863. By that time, each side had lost about 10,000 men.

Union troops took control of Tennessee piece by piece. Tennessee senator Andrew Johnson had remained loyal to the Union. In 1862, President Lincoln made him military governor of Tennessee. He governed the parts of Tennessee seized by the Union. Then, in 1864, Johnson was elected Lincoln's vice-president.

The Union won the Civil War on April 9, 1865. Five days later, President Lincoln was shot. Lincoln died the next morning. Vice-president Andrew Johnson then became the seventeenth president.

A Union artillery piece at Stones River National Cemetery in Murfreesboro

REBUILDING AFTER THE CIVIL WAR

Tennessee had a rough time after the war. Factories, farms, roads, and railroads had to be rebuilt. But Tennesseans showed that they would obey the laws of the United States. Tennessee became the first Confederate state to rejoin the Union.

Many northerners felt that Johnson was too soft on the South. In early 1868, the United States

Many Tennesseans did not want former slaves to be educated or to vote. During riots in Memphis, this Freedman's school was burned.

House of Representatives impeached Johnson. That is, Johnson was accused of doing his job improperly. Andrew Johnson was the only president ever to be impeached. By just one vote, however, the Senate found him not guilty. Johnson was allowed to finish his term as president.

In 1866, some white Tennesseans formed the Ku Klux Klan. These people wore white hoods and robes. They rode around at night terrorizing newly freed slaves. Tennessee passed laws against the Klan in 1869.

In 1878, yellow fever killed 5,200 people in Memphis. That was one of the country's worst yellow fever epidemics.

Tennessee was changing by the late 1880s. It was still mainly a farming state. But growing numbers of Tennesseans were going to work in factories. Textile (cloth) mills were built in Nashville, Knoxville, and Jackson. Lumber, iron, steel, and flour milling grew in importance. Coal mining became important in the East Tennessee mountains.

WORLD WARS, EVOLUTION, AND DEPRESSION

The United States entered World War I (1914-1918) in 1917. Nearly 100,000 Tennesseans volunteered for service. Alvin C. York of Pall Mall was one of the war's great heroes. On October 8, 1918, Sergeant York killed 25 enemy soldiers. He captured 132 others.

The town of Dayton, Tennessee, made world headlines seven years later. Tennessee outlawed the teaching of evolution in 1925. Part of this theory is that people evolved from apelike beings. Dayton teacher John Scopes broke the law. He taught about evolution. He was placed on trial in the summer of 1925. Famous lawyers came to defend and oppose Scopes. The Dayton teacher lost. Not until 1967 did Tennessee allow the teaching of evolution.

A hundred years earlier, Alvin York's great-great-grandfather had hunted with Davy Crockett, a famous Tennessee frontiersman.

Lawyer Clarence Darrow (standing in picture at left) defended John Scopes (right) at what became known as the "Monkey Trial."

The Great Depression hit the United States in 1929. It was a time of great hardship. Many Tennessee businesses and banks closed. Families lost their farms. The United States government began programs to help the country. The Tennessee Valley Authority (TVA) program was begun in 1933. The TVA built dams on the Tennessee River and its branches. The dams helped bring electricity to parts of Tennessee. They also controlled floods. Lakes were created behind the dams.

World War II (1939-1945) helped end the Great Depression. The United States entered the war in 1941. The Volunteer State again lived up to its nickname. More than 315,000 Tennesseans

The Tennessee Valley Authority (TVA) put people to work building dams and locks (above) and planting trees (below).

served. Oak Ridge National Laboratory was built in East Tennessee. There, scientists helped create the atomic bomb. The two atomic bombs that were dropped on Japan in 1945 helped bring the war to an end.

CIVIL RIGHTS

Black Tennesseans had enjoyed their rights for only a short while after the Civil War. By 1890, the state began taking away their rights. This occurred throughout the South. Black southerners were kept from voting. They couldn't go to the same schools or hotels as whites.

The Ku Klux Klan started up again. This hate group spread through the South. Klansmen beat blacks who sought their rights. White people even lynched many southern blacks. Lynchings were hangings done by mobs. About 200 black Tennesseans were lynched between the 1880s and 1950.

The United States government forced the South to end these injustices. The lives of black people started to improve in the 1950s. Tennessee began integrating its schools in 1956. Black children and white children then started attending the same

When Tennessee began integrating its schools in 1956, the National Guard brought in tanks and troops to protect the new black students.

Civil-rights leader Dr. Martin Luther King, Jr. (above) was assassinated in Memphis in 1968.

Other Japanese companies have opened plants in Tennessee.

schools. During the 1960s, voting rights were restored to black Tennesseans. In 1964, A. W. Willis, Jr., was elected to the Tennessee legislature. He was the first black person elected to that body.

In 1968, a great black leader was killed in Tennessee. Dr. Martin Luther King, Jr., was in Memphis. He had come to speak for the rights of the garbage workers. They were on strike. On April 4, King was shot and killed. This assassination took place outside a Memphis motel.

RECENT TRENDS

Through the 1950s and 1960s, industry was booming in Tennessee. Firms that make chemicals, foods, and other goods came to the state. Thousands of farm families moved to the cities. They took jobs in factories. By 1960, more Tennesseans lived in cities than in small towns.

Tennessee became an auto-making center during the 1980s. Two huge car-making plants were built near Nashville. In 1982, the Nissan firm of Japan opened a car-making plant. It is in Smyrna. At that time, it was the costliest foreign project in America. In 1990, General Motors began operating the Saturn auto plant at Spring Hill.

Knoxville hosted a world's fair in 1982. More than 11 million people attended. They poured millions of dollars into the state.

Yet, Tennessee faces big problems today. Many Tennesseans earn less money than people in most other states. By late 1993, 6 percent of all Tennesseans were out of work. The state also has more than its share of people who cannot read.

During the 1990s, Tennessee is working to improve its schools. One of the plans the state began is called the Master Plan for Tennessee Schools: Preparing for the Twenty-first Century. A good education helps people get good jobs. By improving their schools, Tennesseans will enjoy better lives in the future.

The Sunsphere (above) was built for the Tennessee pavilion at the Knoxville World's Fair of 1982.

Overleaf: Knoxville firefighters in front of their truck

Tennesseans and Their Work

TENNESSEANS AND THEIR WORK

Tennessee had nearly 5 million people as of 1990. Only sixteen states had more people. About five of every six Tennesseans are white. About one in six is black. Small numbers of Tennesseans have Hispanic, American Indian, or Asian background.

Gone are the days when most Tennesseans lived in small towns. Six of every ten Tennesseans now live in cities. Two of America's twenty-five largest cities are in Tennessee. They are Memphis and Nashville.

From big cities to small towns, most Tennesseans agree on one thing. They love music. Folk songs and bluegrass music are popular in East Tennessee. Middle Tennessee was the birthplace of country music. The blues and rock and roll started in West Tennessee. Each year many Tennessee towns hold music festivals.

HOW THEY MAKE THEIR LIVING

Almost half a million Tennesseans make products. Thanks to them, Tennessee is a leading manufactur-

Cherokee Indian Heritage Days (above) and several music festivals (below) are among the highlights of the year in Tennessee.

Tennessee is a leading manufacturing state. Some of the items made there are truck tires (left) and guitars (right).

ing state. Chemicals are Tennessee's top products. They range from medicines to soaps. Packaged foods are in second place. These include meats, soft drinks, and breads. Tennessee is a leading car-making state. It is one of the top ten book-publishing states. Sheet music and recordings are other Tennessee products. Tennessee is a leading maker of pencils, carpets, clothing, and shoes. Stoves, furnaces, televisions, radios, and medical instruments are other important products.

More than 450,000 Tennesseans sell goods. About half a million provide services. These people include nurses, lawyers, bankers, and motel workers. A huge service firm has its headquarters in Memphis. It is Federal Express delivery service. About 312,000 Tennesseans do government work.

Tennessee has nearly 90,000 farms. The Volunteer State is a leader at raising beef cattle. Dairy cattle, hogs, and chickens are also important. The Tennessee Walking Horse is raised in the Nashville Basin. Tennessee is also a leading grower of tobacco, cotton, and snap beans. Milk, soybeans, green peas, and tomatoes are other major farm goods.

A few thousand Tennesseans work as miners. The state is a big coal producer. The coal comes from the East Tennessee mountains. Tennessee is also a leading miner of crushed stone. That is used in building roads.

Overleaf: The Nashville skyline

Tennessee farmers grow a variety of produce.

A Trip Through
the Volunteer State

A Trip Through the Volunteer State

Tennessee is a popular vacationland. Nature lovers are drawn to the state's woods and mountains. History lovers come to see its battle-fields and presidents' homes. Millions of music fans come to hear Tennessee's country music.

West Tennessee

Memphis is a good place to start a trip through Tennessee. Memphis lies on the Mississippi River in the state's southwest corner. It is Tennessee's largest city.

The Mississippi River has long been important to the Memphis area. The Indians built villages along the river. Chucalissa Indian Village has been rebuilt. It is about 500 years old. The Mississippi River Museum is at Mud Island in Memphis. It has

Below: A view of the Memphis skyline

displays on steamboats and other river vessels. Many people take cruises on the Mississippi River from Memphis.

In the early 1900s, a new kind of music was born. Memphis's Beale Street area was its birthplace. People called this music "the blues." Composer W. C. Handy is honored as the "Father of the Blues." Handy's home can be visited in the Beale Street Historic District.

In the 1950s, Memphis singer Elvis Presley made rock and roll popular. He cut his first records in Memphis. In 1957, Elvis bought a 23-room home there. It is called Graceland. Each year, Graceland attracts about 600,000 visitors.

About half of all Memphians are black. The National Civil Rights Museum is in Memphis. Its displays show how black people fought for their

Left: A five-block-long scale model of the Mississippi River on Mud Island, in Memphis
Right: The entrance to Graceland, Elvis Presley's home in Memphis

Memphis residents are called Memphians.

rights. The museum is in the motel where Dr. King was assassinated.

Author Alex Haley grew up in Henning, northeast of Memphis. Haley wrote the famous book *Roots: The Saga of an American Family.*

Near Tennessee's northwest corner is Reelfoot Lake. This shallow lake was created by earthquakes in 1811-12. It is a popular place to fish and birdwatch. About 250 kinds of birds have been seen around the lake. Bald eagles winter at Reelfoot Lake.

Kentucky Lake is east of Reelfoot Lake. It is one of the world's biggest artificial lakes. Kentucky Lake is even younger than Reelfoot. It was created by a dam built on the Tennessee River. Part of the lake is in Kentucky. Kentucky Lake is a great vacation area.

West Tennessee is also the site of Shiloh National Military Park. It is on the Tennessee River east of Memphis. One of the bloodiest battles of the Civil War took place there. Today, visitors can tour the battlefield.

MIDDLE TENNESSEE

Nashville is near the center of Tennessee. The Cumberland River winds through downtown

A Confederate monument at Shiloh National Military Park

Nashville. Its river location helped Nashville grow. It is Tennessee's second-largest city.

The capitol, in Nashville

Nashville has been Tennessee's capital since 1826. State lawmakers work in the Tennessee State Capitol. That building was finished in 1859. It is one of the nation's oldest state capitols still in use.

Nashville is called "Music City, USA." No other city is as famous for country music as Nashville. Many famous musicians have recorded along Nashville's Music Row. They include Johnny Cash and Dolly Parton. Music videos for television are also made along Music Row. The Country Music Hall of Fame is there, too.

Above: Grand Ole Opry performers put on a show.

In 1925, a country music show went on the radio from Nashville. The "Grand Ole Opry" is still going today. The "Grand Ole Opry" now broadcasts from Opryland. This is a music theme park outside of Nashville.

Nashville is called the "Athens of the South." Some buildings in the city look like buildings from ancient Athens, Greece. The Parthenon looks like the Greek temple of the same name. Nashville's Parthenon houses an art collection.

The Tennessee State Museum is in Nashville. It covers life in Tennessee from 15,000 years ago to the 1900s. Many old toys are on view at the Nashville Toy Museum. Fort Nashborough has been rebuilt. That fort was built by the first settlers in 1779.

Below: The Parthenon, in Nashville

Just east of Nashville is Andrew Jackson's home, the Hermitage. Jackson and his wife, Rachel, are buried at the Hermitage.

Civil War hero Sam Davis grew up in Smyrna. Davis spied on Union forces. He was captured and hanged in 1863. Davis was only twenty-one. He became known as the "Boy Hero of the Confederacy."

Stones River National Battlefield is near Sam Davis's home. The famous Battle of Murfreesboro was fought there. It is also called the Battle of Stones River.

Tennessee Walking Horses were first developed in Middle Tennessee around 1790. These graceful

The Hermitage (above), outside Nashville, was the home of Andrew Jackson.

horses are still raised in the region. Many Middle Tennessee horse farms welcome visitors.

EAST TENNESSEE

Chattanooga is in the East Tennessee mountains. Lookout Mountain is at the south end of Chattanooga. The world's steepest passenger railroad goes up Lookout Mountain. A Civil War battle was fought on this mountain in 1863. It is called the "Battle above the Clouds."

In the 1940s, there was a popular song about a train. It was called "The Chattanooga Choo-Choo." The original Chattanooga Choo-Choo is displayed at the Chattanooga Choo-Choo Complex.

Lookout Mountain (left) was the site of the Civil War "Battle above the Clouds." The Incline Railway (right) takes passengers up the mountain.

The original Chattanooga Choo-Choo (left) is displayed at the Chattanooga Choo-Choo Complex.

Chattanooga's Tennessee Valley Railroad Museum also has old trains. There, people can even take a trip on one. The Chattanooga African-American Museum is also interesting. It has displays on black history.

Lost Sea Caverns are northeast of Chattanooga. One of the world's largest underground lakes is inside these caves. It is called the Lost Sea. Visitors can explore the lake in a glass-bottomed boat.

East of the Lost Sea is the village of Vonore. The Sequoya Birthplace Museum is there. A few thousand people of Cherokee descent still live in East Tennessee. Their families hid in the mountains to avoid the "Trail of Tears."

America's most popular national park is east of Sequoya's birthplace. This is Great Smoky

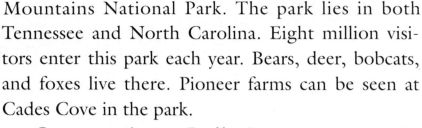

The Great Smokies are part of the Appalachian Mountains. They were given their name because mist and clouds give them a smoky look.

Mountains National Park. The park lies in both Tennessee and North Carolina. Eight million visitors enter this park each year. Bears, deer, bobcats, and foxes live there. Pioneer farms can be seen at Cades Cove in the park.

Country singer Dolly Parton grew up in Sevierville. Halfway between Sevierville and the Great Smokies is Pigeon Forge. In 1986, Parton opened an amusement park called Dollywood in Pigeon Forge.

Knoxville is northwest of Pigeon Forge. James White and his family settled Knoxville in 1786. Their log cabin and fort can be visited. Knoxville is Tennessee's third-largest city. It was Tennessee's capital in the late 1700s and early 1800s. The Blount Mansion is in Knoxville. William Blount was governor of the Tennessee Territory.

Oak Ridge is a short drive west of Knoxville. Scientists at Oak Ridge National Laboratory helped build the atomic bomb. Today, Oak Ridge people work on peaceful uses for atomic energy. Oak Ridge's American Museum of Science and Energy helps explain this work.

The Museum of Appalachia is a village near Norris. Twenty-five old log buildings have been brought there. Those buildings are filled with items

Krutch Park, in Knoxville

The Old Mill, at
Pigeon Forge

from pioneer days. The village also has a working Tennessee mountain farm.

Greeneville is east of Norris. Andrew Johnson moved to Greeneville when he was seventeen. Johnson's home and the tailor shop where he worked can be visited.

Davy Crockett was born near Limestone, on the banks of the Nolichucky River. The cabin where he was born has been rebuilt. It is in Davy Crockett Birthplace Park near Limestone.

Tennessee's oldest town is a good place to end a Tennessee trip. This is Jonesborough, north of Limestone. Andrew Jackson tried his first cases as a lawyer in Jonesborough. Many buildings that Jackson knew still stand in the town. Today, the National Storytelling Festival takes place each October in Jonesborough.

The Museun of
Appalachia, near
Norris

A Gallery of Famous Tennesseans

A GALLERY OF FAMOUS TENNESSEANS

Tennessee has produced many famous people. The state has become home to many others. Tennesseans have played important roles in the country's history. Today, many Tennesseans are known throughout the world. Their music has made them famous.

Sequoya (1760?-1843) was born in the East Tennessee mountains. Around 1809, Sequoya began work on a Cherokee alphabet. The great Cherokee leader finished it twelve years later. Sequoya proved his alphabet's value. Thousands of Cherokees learned to read using Sequoya's letters.

Cherokee leader Sequoya

Andrew Jackson (1767-1845) was born in South Carolina. He served in the Revolutionary War when he was only thirteen. At twenty-one, Jackson moved to Tennessee. He became a lawyer. He served in the U.S. House of Representatives (1796-1797) and the Senate (1797-1798, 1823-1825). Jackson was a hero in the War of 1812. In 1828, "Old Hickory" won election as president. He was reelected in 1832.

Andrew Johnson (1808-1875) was born in North Carolina. When he was seventeen, he moved

Andrew Jackson earned the nickname "Old Hickory" because people said he was as tough as hickory wood

Opposite: Davy Crockett

*Left: President
Andrew Johnson
Right: Admiral David
Farragut*

to Tennessee. Later, he became a famous politician. Johnson spoke against joining the Confederacy. He was the only southern U.S. senator to do that. In 1864, Johnson was elected vice-president. The next year, he became president after Lincoln was assassinated.

David "Davy" Crockett (1786-1836) was born near Limestone. He became a famous bear hunter and storyteller. Tennesseans elected Crockett to the U.S. Congress (1827-1831, 1833-1835). Crockett took an unpopular stand. He didn't want the Indians moved off their land. This helped defeat him in his run for Congress in 1834. Crockett then went to Texas. He died at the Alamo fighting to free Texas from Mexico.

Samuel "Sam" Houston (1793 1863) grew up in Tennessee. Houston ran away from home when he was about fifteen. He lived with the Cherokees for three years. Later, he taught school and fought under Andrew Jackson. In 1827, Houston was elected governor of Tennessee. But when his wife left him, he quit. He returned to the Cherokees. Later, Houston moved to Texas. He led the army that freed Texas from Mexico in 1836.

David Farragut (1801-1870) was born near Knoxville. Farragut joined the navy at the age of nine. He served under the navy captain who adopted him. During the War of 1812, Farragut commanded a captured ship. He was only twelve years old at the time! Fifty years later, Farragut helped the Union win the Civil War. In 1866, he became the first U.S. Navy admiral.

Robert R. Church (1839-1912) was born a slave. His mother, also a slave, died when Church was twelve. Church then went to work for his father. His father was a white riverboat captain based in Memphis. Church washed dishes on the boat. By the end of the Civil War, Church had gained his freedom. He bought property in

Soldier and politician Sam Houston

Statesman Cordell Hull

Physician and politician Dorothy Brown

Memphis with his savings. He became very rich. Church helped develop Beale Street. He also founded a bank.

Ida B. Wells (1862-1931) was born a slave. She was freed as a young child. In 1884, she moved to Memphis. There, she taught school. She also became part owner of a newspaper. In 1892, a Memphis mob lynched three of her friends. Wells launched a campaign against lynching. She also demanded that black Americans be granted their other rights. Ida B. Wells was one of the first civil-rights workers.

Cordell Hull (1871-1955) was born near Byrdstown. He became a famous statesman. Hull was U.S. secretary of state from 1933 to 1944. He played a big role in the birth of the United Nations. Hull won the 1945 Nobel Peace Prize for his work.

Dorothy Brown was born in 1919. She spent her first thirteen years in an orphanage. Later, she became a famous surgeon in Nashville. She also taught at Meharry Medical College in Nashville. Then, Dr. Brown entered politics. In 1966, she was elected to the Tennessee legislature. Brown became the first black woman to serve in that body.

Tennessee has also produced many great musicians. **Bessie Smith** (1894?-1937) was born in

Chattanooga. By the age of nine, she was singing on Chattanooga's streets. She sang for pennies. A few years later, she joined a traveling music show. Bessie Smith became one of the greatest blues singers of all time.

Elvis Presley (1935-1977) moved to Memphis when he was thirteen. One day in 1953, he stopped at a Memphis recording studio. He made a record of his singing as a gift for his mother. People loved the way Presley sounded. He soon became famous. Presley became known as the "King of Rock and Roll." He also made 33 movies.

Dolly Parton was born near Sevierville in 1946. She was the fourth of twelve children. Dolly's

Elvis Presley had a twin brother who died at birth.

Left: Blues singer Bessie Smith
Right: Rock-and-roll king, Elvis Presley

Country singer, songwriter, movie star, and theme-park owner Dolly Parton

family sang together for fun. Parton made up her first song when she was five years old. Her mother wrote it down on a paper bag. Dolly Parton is now a famous country singer, songwriter, and movie star.

The list of famous Tennessee-born singers goes on. **Roy Acuff** (1903-1992) was born in Maynardville. He was known as the "King of Country Music." **Aretha Franklin** was born in Memphis in 1942. She is the "Queen of Soul Music." **Tennessee Ernie Ford** (1919-1991) was born in Bristol. In 1955, Ford recorded "Sixteen Tons." It was one of the best-selling records of all time. Singer **Tina Turner** was born in 1939 in Brownsville. Opera star **Grace Moore** (1901-1947) was born near Newport.

Famous athletes have also come from Tennessee. **Cary Middlecoff** was born in 1921 in Halls. He had two careers. He became a dentist and a pro golfer. Dr. Cary Middlecoff won the 1955 Masters Tournament and the 1949 and 1956 U.S. Open tournaments.

Wilma Rudolph (1940-1994) was born near Clarksville. When she was four, Rudolph lost the use of one leg. This happened after an illness. Family members took turns rubbing the leg. Finally, at the age of eight, Rudolph could walk. Soon, she was not only walking but running very fast. In the 1960

Both soul-music singer Aretha Franklin (left) and golfer Cary Middlecoff (right) are native Tennesseans.

Olympics, Rudolph won three gold medals. She was the first U.S. woman runner to do that.

The birthplace of Wilma Rudolph, Davy Crockett, Bessie Smith, Sequoya, and Dolly Parton . . .

Home to Andrew Jackson, Elvis Presley, Sam Houston, and Ida B. Wells . . .

The site of the Grand Ole Opry, Lookout Mountain, Reelfoot Lake, and the Hermitage . . .

The place where the Watauga Association was formed and where the Battle of Shiloh was fought . . .

This is the Volunteer State—Tennessee!

Did You Know?

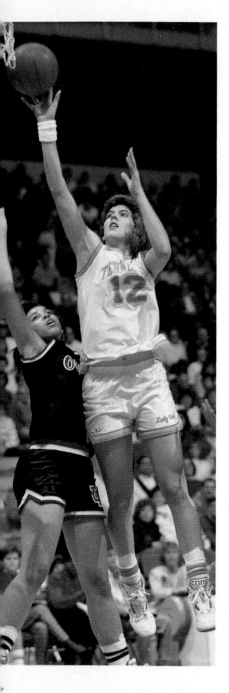

The University of Tennessee Lady Volunteers won the 1987, 1989, and 1991 women's national college basketball championships.

Roy Acuff suffered sunstroke at a New York Yankee baseball camp. Otherwise, he might have become a baseball player instead of the "King of Country Music."

East Tennessee has two "champion" trees. Cocke County has the nation's biggest pecan tree. Its trunk is 19 feet around, and its height is 143 feet. The nation's champion yellow buckeye is in Great Smoky Mountains National Park. Its trunk is 18 feet around, and its height is 145 feet.

During her second year of high school, Wilma Rudolph scored 803 points in 25 basketball games. This set a Tennessee high-school scoring record for girls.

Tennessee has towns named Bell Buckle, Bells, Finger, Ducktown, Friendship, Bean Station, Bone Cave, Difficult, Only, Christmasville, Skullbone, and Wartburg.

***Roots,* by Alex Haley, became an eight-part television series in 1977. The last part was one of the most-watched shows in United States television history. More than 35 million households tuned in to watch it.**

Tennessee has about 4,000 known caves.

Alf Taylor was seventy-five years old when he left office as governor in 1923. He was Tennessee's oldest governor.

Major-league baseball didn't allow black players until 1947. Before then, blacks played in the "Negro leagues." There were many great players in those leagues. For example, one of the greatest pitchers of all time played for the Nashville Elite Giants and the Chattanooga Black Lookouts. His name was Satchel Paige.

Several Tennessee libraries hold worm races as part of their summer reading programs. The races help turn the children into "bookworms." The Johnson City Public Library began this custom in Tennessee.

Tennessee Information

State flag

Iris

Firefly

Area: 42,114 square miles (thirty-fourth among the states in size)

Greatest Distance North to South: 116 miles

Greatest Distance East to West: 482 miles

Borders: Kentucky and Virginia to the north; North Carolina to the east; Georgia, Alabama, and Mississippi to the south; Arkansas and Missouri to the west

Highest Point: Clingmans Dome, 6,643 feet above sea level

Lowest Point: 182 feet above sea level, near Memphis,

Hottest Recorded Temperature: 113° F. (at Perryville, on both July 29 and August 9, 1930)

Coldest Recorded Temperature: -32° F. (at Mountain City, on December 30, 1917)

Statehood: The sixteenth state, on June 1, 1796

Origin of Name: Tennessee was named for *Tanasie*, a Cherokee Indian village

Capital: Nashville (since 1826)

Previous Capitals: Knoxville (1792-1812, 1817), Nashville (1812-1817), Murfreesboro (1818-1826)

Counties: 95

United States Representatives: 9 (as of 1992)

State Senators: 33

State Representatives: 99

State Songs: Since Tennessee is such a musical state, it has not one but five state songs: "My Homeland, Tennessee," by Nell Grayson Taylor (words) and Roy Lamont Smith (music); "When It's Iris Time in Tennessee," by Willa Mae Ward; "My Tennessee," by Francis Hannah Tranum; "The Tennessee Waltz," by Pee Wee King (words) and Redd Stewart (music); "Rocky Top," by Boudleaux and Felice Bryant

State Motto: "Agriculture and Commerce"

Main Nickname: "Volunteer State"

Other Nickname: "Big Bend State"

State Seal: Adopted in 1801

State Flag: Adopted in 1905

State Flower: Iris

State Wildflower: Passionflower

State Bird: Mockingbird

State Tree: Tulip poplar

State Animal: Raccoon

State Horse: Tennessee Walking Horse

State Insects: Firefly and ladybug

State Gem: Tennessee River pearls

Main Rivers: Mississippi, Tennessee, Cumberland

Wildlife: Bears, deer, rabbits, raccoons, foxes, beavers, mockingbirds, cardinals, robins, bluebirds, eagles, many other kinds of birds, catfish, bass, trout, many other kinds of fish

Manufactured Products: Chemicals, food products, cars, stoves, home furnaces, air conditioners, carpeting, clothing, other cloth goods, shoes, books, pencils, plastic materials, tires, televisions, radios, medical instruments, furniture

Farm Products: Beef cattle, hogs, chickens, Tennessee Walking Horses, eggs, soybeans, milk, tobacco, cotton, green peas, tomatoes, snap beans, apples, peaches, corn, wheat

Mining Products: Coal, crushed stone, zinc, marble, limestone, copper, clay

Population: 4,877,185, seventeenth among the fifty states (1990 U.S. Census Bureau figures)

Major Cities (1990 Census):

Memphis	610,337	Clarksville	75,494
Nashville	488,374	Johnson City	49,381
Knoxville	165,121	Jackson	48,949
Chattanooga	152,466	Murfreesboro	44,922

Tennessee Walking Horse

Tulip poplar blossom

Raccoon

Tennessee History

13,000 B.C.—Indians reach Tennessee

A.D. 1500—The Cherokees and Chickasaws are living in Tennessee

1540—Spanish explorer Hernando De Soto explores Tennessee

1673—James Needham and Gabriel Arthur explore Tennessee for England; Louis Jolliet and Father Jacques Marquette reach Tennessee while canoeing down the Mississippi River

1682—French explorer René-Robert Cavelier, Sieur de La Salle, builds Fort Prudhomme in southwestern Tennessee

1714—French trader Charles Charleville starts a trading post at present-day Nashville

1750—Dr. Thomas Walker discovers the Cumberland Gap

1763—England wins the French and Indian War and lands east of the Mississippi River; Tennessee is part of North Carolina

1769—William Bean builds a cabin near the Watauga River

1772—The Watauga Association is formed and adopts one of the first documents for self-government in North America

1775—Daniel Boone blazes the Wilderness Road

1779—Jonesborough becomes Tennessee's first organized town

1789—North Carolina turns Tennessee over to the U.S. government, which makes it a U.S. territory

1796—Tennessee becomes the sixteenth state on June 1

1800—Tennessee's population is 105,602

1811-12—Earthquakes create Reelfoot Lake

1818—The Chickasaws sell their West Tennessee lands to the U.S. government

1826—Davy Crockett is elected to the U.S. Congress

1828—Andrew Jackson is elected the seventh U.S. president

1838-39—Most Cherokees are forced from Tennessee to lands in Oklahoma

The first territorial capitol

1844—James K. Polk is elected the eleventh U.S. president

1860—Abraham Lincoln is elected president

1861—The Civil War begins on April 12; on June 8, Tennessee becomes the last of eleven states to leave the Union

1862—At the Battle of Shiloh, 24,000 troops are killed or wounded

1862-63—At the Battle of Murfreesboro, 20,000 are killed or wounded

1864—Andrew Johnson is elected vice-president

1865—The Confederacy loses the Civil War; President Lincoln is assassinated; Johnson becomes president

1866—On July 24, Tennessee becomes the first Confederate state to rejoin the Union

1878—Yellow fever kills 5,200 people in Memphis

1900—The population of Tennessee is 2,020,616

1917-18—After the United States enters World War I, nearly 100,000 Tennesseans volunteer; Sergeant Alvin C. York receives the Medal of Honor

1925—The Scopes "Monkey Trial" is held in Dayton, Tennessee

1933—The U.S. Congress creates the Tennessee Valley Authority

1941-45—More than 315,000 Tennesseans help win World War II; workers at Oak Ridge National Laboratory help create the atomic bomb

1964—A. W. Willis, Jr., becomes the first black person elected to the Tennessee legislature during the 1900s

1968—Dr. Martin Luther King, Jr., is assassinated in Memphis

1972—Opryland USA, a theme park, opens in Nashville

1982—Knoxville hosts a world's fair

1990—Tennessee's population reaches 4,877,185

1994—Tennessee becomes the 18th state to permit adults to carry concealed handguns

A Civil War reenactment at Stones River National Battlefield and Cemetery

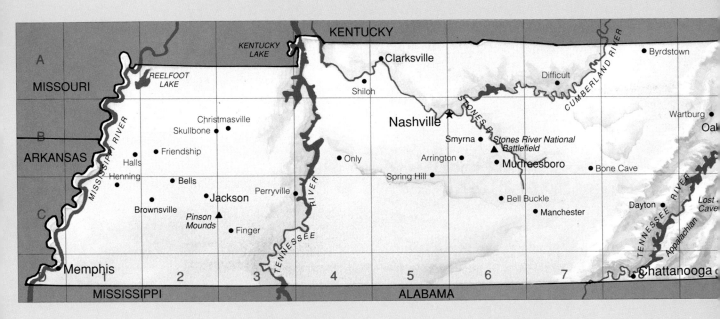

MAP KEY

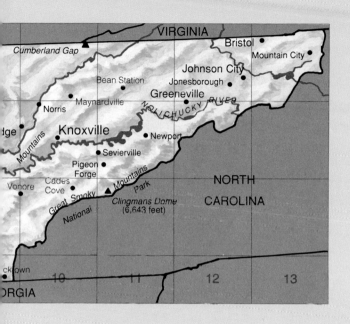

GLOSSARY

ancient: Relating to a time early in history

assassinate: To murder someone who is in politics or government, usually by a secret or sudden attack

artificial: Made by people rather than occurring naturally

astronomer: A person who studies the stars, planets, and other heavenly bodies

blues: A kind of music that often expresses sadness; the blues developed in the Beale Street area of Memphis in the early 1900s

capital: The city that is the seat of government

capitol: The building in which the government meets

century: A period of 100 years

climate: The typical weather of a region

colony: A settlement that is outside a parent country and that is ruled by the parent country

disaster: A terrible event, often with much suffering and death

epidemic: A big outbreak of a disease

61

explorer: A person who visits and studies unknown lands

impeach: To charge a public official with misconduct

independence: Being free from the control of others and able to take care of one's self

integrate: To bring different races of people, such as black people and white people, together in the same schools, neighborhoods, and jobs

slave: A person who is owned by another person

territory: Land that is not yet a state but is under the control of the U.S. government

tornado: A violent windstorm with a funnel-shaped cloud that travels over land causing great destruction

universe: All of space and everything that is in it

PICTURE ACKNOWLEDGMENTS

Front cover, © **Matt Bradley;** 1, © **Clemenz Photography;** 2, **Tom Dunnington;** 3, © Frank Siteman/**NE Stock Photo;** 4-5, **Tom Dunnington;** 6-7, © T. Algire/**H. Armstrong Roberts;** 8, **courtesy of Hammond, Incorporated, Maplewood, New Jersey;** 9 (left), © H. Abernathy/**H. Armstrong Roberts;** 9 (right), © Willard Clay/**Tony Stone Worldwide/Chicago, Ltd.;** 10, © Willard Clay/**Tony Stone Worldwide/Chicago, Ltd.;** 11 (left), © H. Abernathy/**H. Armstrong Roberts;** 11 (right), © Bob Brudd/**Tony Stone Worldwide/Chicago, Ltd.;** 12 (top left), © **Jamie Adams;** 12 (top right), © B.Kulik/ **Photri;** 12 (bottom), © Michael & Elvan Habicht/**Photri;** 13, © Michael Hubrich/**Dembinsky Photo Assoc.;** 14, © H. Abernathy/**H. Armstrong Roberts;** 16, **Historical Pictures/Stock Montage;** 17, **Historical Pictures/Stock Montage;** 18, **North Wind Picture Archives, hand colored;** 19 (left), **Historical Pictures/Stock Montage;** 19 (right), **courtesy Tennessee State Museum, Tennessee Historical Society Collection, photograph by June Dorman;** 20, © Donald Smetzer/**Tony Stone Worldwide/Chicago, Ltd.;** 21, **Historical Pictures/Stock Montage;** 22, **Library of Congress;** 23, © W.J. Scott/**H. Armstrong Roberts;** 24, **Historical Pictures/Stock Montage;** 25 (left), **UPI/Bettmann Newsphotos;** 25 (right), **AP/Wide World Photos;** 26 (top), **AP/Wide World Photos;** 26 (bottom), **Historical Pictures/Stock Montage;** 27, **AP/Wide World Photos;** 28, **AP/Wide World Photos;** 29, © **Photri;** 30, © **Matt Bradley;** 31 (top), © **Jeff Isaac Greenberg;** 31 (bottom), © Frank Siteman/**NE Stock Photo;** 32 (both pictures), © **Cameramann International, Ltd.;** 33, © I. MacDonald/**Root Resources;** 34-35, © Bill Ross/**H. Armstrong Roberts;** 36, © Mark Segal/**Tony Stone Worldwide/Chicago, Ltd.;** 37 (left), © R.Krubner/**H. Armstrong Roberts;** 37 (right), © **Joan Dunlop;** 38, © **Tom Till/Photographer;** 39, © R. Krubner/**H. Armstrong Roberts;** 40 (top), © Don Smetzer/**Tony Stone Worldwide/Chicago, Ltd.;** 40 (bottom), © W. J. Scott/**H. Armstrong Roberts;** 41, © **William Schemmel;** 42 (left), © **Tom and Joanne O'Toole;** 42 (right), © Richard L. Capps/**R/C Photo Agency;** 43, © **William Schemmel Photo;** 44, © **Photri;** 45 (both pictures), © **Clemenz Photography;** 46, © **Photri;** 47, **Historical Pictures/Stock Montage;** 48 (left), **North Wind Picture Archives;** 48 (right), **AP/Wide World Photos;** 49, **Historical Pictures/Stock Montage;** 50 (top), **Historical Pictures/Stock Montage;** 50 (bottom), **AP/Wide World Photos;** 51 (both pictures), **AP/Wide World Photos;** 52, **AP/Wide World Photos;** 53 (both pictures), **AP/Wide World Photos;** 54, **University of Tennessee/Tennessee Women's Athletic Department;** 55 (top), © **James P. Rowan;** 55 (bottom), **National Baseball Hall of Fame and Museum, Inc.;** 56 (top), **courtesy Flag Research Center, Winchester, Massachusetts 01890;** 56 (middle), © Lani/**Photri;** 56 (bottom), © **Photri;** 57 (top), © **Tennessee Tourist Bureau;** 57 (middle), © Kitty Kohout/**Root Resources;** 57 (bottom), © Richard L.Capps/**R/C Photo Agency;** 58, © H. Abernathy/ **H. Armstrong Roberts;** 59, © **Mack & Betty Kelley;** 60-61, **Tom Dunnington;** back cover, © Mark Reinholz/ **Marilyn Gartman Agency**

INDEX

Page numbers in boldface type indicate illustrations.

ABOUT THE AUTHOR

Dennis Brindell Fradin is the author of 150 published children's books. His works for Childrens Press include the Young People's Stories of Our States series, the Disaster! series, and the Thirteen Colonies series. Dennis is married to Judith Bloom Fradin, who taught high-school and college English for many years. She is now Dennis's chief researcher. The Fradins are the parents of two sons, Anthony and Michael, and a daughter, Diana. Dennis graduated from Northwestern University in 1967 with a B.A. in creative writing, and has lived in Evanston, Illinois, since that year.